50 The Art of the Morning Table Recipes

By: Kelly Johnson

Table of Contents

- Fluffy Buttermilk Pancakes
- Classic French Toast
- Savory Avocado Toast with Poached Eggs
- Honey-Glazed Croissants
- Maple Pecan Oatmeal
- Bacon and Cheddar Scones
- Greek Yogurt Parfaits with Berries
- Spinach and Feta Breakfast Strata
- Cinnamon Swirl Coffee Cake
- Ham and Gruyere Breakfast Casserole
- Cranberry Orange Muffins
- Mushroom and Herb Frittata
- Lemon Ricotta Pancakes
- Cheddar Biscuits with Sausage Gravy
- Banana Nut Bread
- Roasted Vegetable Breakfast Hash
- Chive and Cream Cheese Bagels
- Breakfast Burritos with Salsa
- Eggs Benedict with Hollandaise Sauce
- Smoked Salmon and Dill Crepes
- Apple Cinnamon Dutch Baby
- Blueberry Lemon Scones
- Caramelized Onion and Goat Cheese Quiche
- Sweet Potato and Kale Hash
- Maple Bacon Waffles
- Chorizo and Egg Tacos
- Chocolate Chip Banana Pancakes
- Green Smoothie Bowl
- Ricotta and Honey Toast with Pistachios
- Savory Cheese and Herb Muffins
- Mango Coconut Chia Pudding
- Almond Croissant Bread Pudding
- Cheesy Potato Breakfast Skillet
- Breakfast Pizza with Arugula
- Cranberry Walnut Bagels

- Breakfast Tacos with Avocado Crema
- Zucchini and Parmesan Mini Frittatas
- Carrot Cake Oatmeal
- Turkey Sausage and Spinach Wraps
- Almond Butter and Berry Breakfast Toast
- Gingerbread Waffles with Whipped Cream
- Vegan Breakfast Burritos
- Sweet Corn and Cheddar Muffins
- Pear and Almond Danish
- Scrambled Tofu Breakfast Bowl
- Coconut Milk Rice Porridge with Mango
- Hearty Lentil and Kale Breakfast Soup
- Pistachio and Raspberry Overnight Oats
- Classic Bagel and Lox Platter
- Chocolate Hazelnut Crepes

Fluffy Buttermilk Pancakes

Ingredients:

- 2 cups all-purpose flour
- 2 tbsp granulated sugar
- 2 tsp baking powder
- 1/2 tsp baking soda
- 1/2 tsp salt
- 2 cups buttermilk
- 2 large eggs
- 1/4 cup unsalted butter, melted (plus extra for greasing)
- 1 tsp vanilla extract

Instructions:

1. In a large bowl, whisk together flour, sugar, baking powder, baking soda, and salt.
2. In another bowl, whisk together buttermilk, eggs, melted butter, and vanilla extract.
3. Pour the wet ingredients into the dry ingredients and stir until just combined (batter will be lumpy).
4. Heat a griddle or nonstick skillet over medium heat and lightly grease with butter.
5. Scoop about 1/4 cup of batter onto the griddle for each pancake. Cook until bubbles form on the surface and the edges look set, about 2-3 minutes.
6. Flip and cook for another 1-2 minutes, until golden brown.
7. Serve warm with your favorite toppings.

Classic French Toast

Ingredients:

- 4 slices of thick bread (brioche or challah recommended)
- 2 large eggs
- 1/2 cup whole milk
- 1 tsp vanilla extract
- 1/2 tsp ground cinnamon
- 1 tbsp unsalted butter
- Maple syrup and powdered sugar, for serving
  Instructions:
1. In a shallow dish, whisk together eggs, milk, vanilla, and cinnamon.
2. Heat butter in a skillet over medium heat.
3. Dip each bread slice into the egg mixture, ensuring both sides are well coated.
4. Place the bread slices in the skillet and cook until golden brown, about 2-3 minutes per side.
5. Serve warm with maple syrup and a dusting of powdered sugar.

Savory Avocado Toast with Poached Eggs

Ingredients:

- 2 slices of sourdough bread
- 1 ripe avocado, mashed
- 2 large eggs
- 1 tbsp white vinegar
- Salt and pepper, to taste
- Red pepper flakes, for garnish
- Fresh herbs (optional, for garnish)

Instructions:

1. Toast the sourdough slices until golden and crispy.
2. Spread mashed avocado evenly over each slice, and season with salt and pepper.
3. Bring a pot of water to a gentle simmer and add vinegar. Crack each egg into a small dish and carefully slide it into the water. Poach for 3-4 minutes.
4. Use a slotted spoon to remove the eggs and place one on each avocado toast.
5. Garnish with red pepper flakes and fresh herbs if desired.

Honey-Glazed Croissants

Ingredients:

- 4 store-bought croissants (or homemade)
- 2 tbsp honey
- 1 tbsp unsalted butter
- A pinch of sea salt
  Instructions:
1. Preheat the oven to 350°F (175°C).
2. Place croissants on a baking sheet and warm them in the oven for 5 minutes.
3. In a small saucepan, melt butter over low heat and stir in honey and sea salt.
4. Brush the warm croissants generously with the honey glaze.
5. Serve immediately, with extra honey on the side if desired.

Maple Pecan Oatmeal

Ingredients:

- 1 cup rolled oats
- 2 cups milk or water
- 1/4 cup maple syrup
- 1/4 cup chopped pecans
- 1/2 tsp cinnamon
- Pinch of salt

Instructions:

1. In a saucepan, bring milk or water to a simmer.
2. Stir in oats, cinnamon, and salt. Cook for 5 minutes, stirring occasionally.
3. Remove from heat and stir in maple syrup and pecans.
4. Serve warm, garnished with extra pecans and a drizzle of maple syrup.

Bacon and Cheddar Scones

Ingredients:

- 2 cups all-purpose flour
- 1 tbsp baking powder
- 1/2 tsp salt
- 1/4 cup cold unsalted butter, cubed
- 1/2 cup cooked, crumbled bacon
- 1/2 cup shredded cheddar cheese
- 3/4 cup heavy cream

Instructions:

1. Preheat oven to 400°F (200°C) and line a baking sheet with parchment paper.
2. In a bowl, whisk together flour, baking powder, and salt. Cut in butter until crumbly.
3. Stir in bacon and cheddar, then add cream to form a dough.
4. Shape into a disc, cut into wedges, and place on the baking sheet.
5. Bake for 15-20 minutes, until golden brown.

Greek Yogurt Parfaits with Berries

Ingredients:

- 2 cups Greek yogurt
- 1 cup granola
- 1 cup mixed fresh berries (strawberries, blueberries, raspberries)
- 2 tbsp honey
  Instructions:
1. In glasses or bowls, layer yogurt, granola, and berries.
2. Drizzle with honey and serve immediately.

Spinach and Feta Breakfast Strata

Ingredients:

- 6 cups cubed bread (day-old preferred)
- 2 cups fresh spinach, chopped
- 1 cup crumbled feta cheese
- 6 large eggs
- 2 cups milk
- Salt and pepper, to taste

Instructions:

1. Grease a baking dish and layer bread, spinach, and feta.
2. In a bowl, whisk together eggs, milk, salt, and pepper. Pour over the bread mixture.
3. Cover and refrigerate overnight or let sit for at least 30 minutes.
4. Preheat oven to 350°F (175°C) and bake for 45-50 minutes, until golden and set.

Cinnamon Swirl Coffee Cake

Ingredients:

- 2 cups all-purpose flour
- 1 cup sugar
- 1 tsp baking powder
- 1/2 tsp baking soda
- 1/2 tsp salt
- 1 cup sour cream
- 2 large eggs
- 1/2 cup unsalted butter, melted
- 1/2 cup brown sugar
- 1 tbsp cinnamon

Instructions:

1. Preheat oven to 350°F (175°C) and grease a 9-inch baking pan.
2. In a bowl, mix flour, sugar, baking powder, baking soda, and salt.
3. In another bowl, whisk sour cream, eggs, and melted butter. Combine with the dry ingredients.
4. In a separate bowl, mix brown sugar and cinnamon. Pour half the batter into the pan, sprinkle with the cinnamon mixture, and top with remaining batter.
5. Bake for 35-40 minutes.

Ham and Gruyere Breakfast Casserole

Ingredients:

- 6 cups cubed bread
- 2 cups diced ham
- 1 1/2 cups shredded Gruyere cheese
- 6 large eggs
- 2 cups milk
- Salt and pepper, to taste
  Instructions:
1. Grease a baking dish and layer bread, ham, and cheese.
2. In a bowl, whisk eggs, milk, salt, and pepper. Pour over the bread mixture.
3. Cover and refrigerate overnight or let sit for 30 minutes.
4. Preheat oven to 350°F (175°C) and bake for 45-50 minutes.

Cranberry Orange Muffins

Ingredients:

- 2 cups all-purpose flour
- 3/4 cup sugar
- 2 tsp baking powder
- 1/2 tsp salt
- 1/2 cup fresh cranberries, chopped
- Zest of 1 orange
- 2 large eggs
- 1/2 cup milk
- 1/3 cup vegetable oil

Instructions:

1. Preheat oven to 375°F (190°C) and line a muffin tin.
2. In a bowl, mix flour, sugar, baking powder, salt, cranberries, and orange zest.
3. In another bowl, whisk eggs, milk, and oil. Combine with the dry ingredients.
4. Spoon into the muffin tin and bake for 20-25 minutes.

Mushroom and Herb Frittata

Ingredients:

- 1 tbsp olive oil
- 1 cup sliced mushrooms
- 6 large eggs
- 1/4 cup milk
- 1/4 cup chopped fresh herbs (parsley, chives, or dill)
- Salt and pepper, to taste
- 1/4 cup grated Parmesan cheese
  Instructions:
1. Preheat oven to 375°F (190°C).
2. Heat olive oil in an ovenproof skillet and sauté mushrooms until tender.
3. In a bowl, whisk eggs, milk, herbs, salt, and pepper. Pour over the mushrooms.
4. Sprinkle with Parmesan and bake for 15-20 minutes, until set.

Lemon Ricotta Pancakes

Ingredients:

- 1 cup ricotta cheese
- 2 large eggs, separated
- 1 cup all-purpose flour
- 1/2 cup milk
- 2 tbsp granulated sugar
- 1 tsp baking powder
- Zest of 1 lemon
- Butter, for cooking

Instructions:

1. In a bowl, whisk together ricotta, egg yolks, milk, sugar, and lemon zest.
2. Fold in flour and baking powder until just combined.
3. In another bowl, beat egg whites until stiff peaks form, then gently fold into the batter.
4. Heat a skillet over medium heat, melt butter, and cook pancakes for 2-3 minutes per side.

Cheddar Biscuits with Sausage Gravy

Ingredients:

- 2 cups all-purpose flour
- 1 tbsp baking powder
- 1/2 tsp salt
- 1/4 cup cold unsalted butter, cubed
- 1 cup shredded cheddar cheese
- 3/4 cup milk
- 1 lb ground sausage
- 2 tbsp all-purpose flour
- 2 cups whole milk
- Salt and pepper, to taste

Instructions:

1. Preheat oven to 425°F (220°C). Mix flour, baking powder, and salt. Cut in butter, stir in cheddar, and add milk to form a dough. Drop onto a baking sheet and bake for 12-15 minutes.
2. Cook sausage in a skillet, sprinkle with flour, and stir. Gradually add milk, stirring, until thickened. Season with salt and pepper. Serve over biscuits.

Banana Nut Bread

Ingredients:

- 3 ripe bananas, mashed
- 1/2 cup unsalted butter, melted
- 3/4 cup sugar
- 2 large eggs
- 1 1/2 cups all-purpose flour
- 1 tsp baking soda
- 1/2 tsp salt
- 1/2 cup chopped nuts (walnuts or pecans)

Instructions:

1. Preheat oven to 350°F (175°C) and grease a loaf pan.
2. Mix bananas, butter, sugar, and eggs. Add flour, baking soda, and salt, then fold in nuts.
3. Pour into the pan and bake for 50-60 minutes.

Roasted Vegetable Breakfast Hash

Ingredients:

- 2 cups diced potatoes
- 1 cup diced bell peppers
- 1/2 cup diced onion
- 1 cup zucchini, diced
- 2 tbsp olive oil
- Salt and pepper, to taste
- 4 large eggs

Instructions:

1. Preheat oven to 425°F (220°C). Toss vegetables with olive oil, salt, and pepper.
2. Spread on a baking sheet and roast for 20-25 minutes.
3. Crack eggs over the vegetables and bake for another 8-10 minutes, until eggs are set.

Chive and Cream Cheese Bagels

Ingredients:

- 4 bagels, sliced
- 1/2 cup cream cheese
- 2 tbsp chopped fresh chives
  Instructions:
1. Mix cream cheese and chives.
2. Spread onto bagel halves and serve.

Breakfast Burritos with Salsa

Ingredients:

- 4 large flour tortillas
- 4 large eggs, scrambled
- 1 cup cooked sausage or bacon
- 1 cup shredded cheddar cheese
- 1/2 cup salsa
  Instructions:
1. Warm tortillas and layer with scrambled eggs, sausage, cheese, and salsa.
2. Roll up and serve warm.

Eggs Benedict with Hollandaise Sauce

Ingredients:

- 4 English muffins, halved and toasted
- 8 slices of Canadian bacon
- 4 large eggs
- 1/2 cup unsalted butter, melted
- 2 large egg yolks
- 1 tbsp lemon juice
- Salt and cayenne pepper, to taste

Instructions:

1. Poach eggs in simmering water.
2. In a blender, mix egg yolks, lemon juice, salt, and cayenne. Slowly drizzle in melted butter to form hollandaise.
3. Assemble muffins with bacon, poached eggs, and hollandaise sauce.

Smoked Salmon and Dill Crepes

Ingredients:

- 1 cup all-purpose flour
- 2 large eggs
- 1 1/4 cups milk
- 2 tbsp melted butter
- 1/2 cup cream cheese
- 4 oz smoked salmon
- 1 tbsp fresh dill, chopped
  Instructions:
1. Whisk together flour, eggs, milk, and butter to form a batter. Cook thin crepes in a nonstick skillet.
2. Spread cream cheese on each crepe, top with salmon and dill, then roll up and serve.

Apple Cinnamon Dutch Baby

Ingredients:

- 2 large eggs
- 1/2 cup milk
- 1/2 cup all-purpose flour
- 1 tbsp sugar
- 1/2 tsp cinnamon
- Pinch of salt
- 1 tbsp butter
- 1 apple, thinly sliced
- Powdered sugar, for serving

Instructions:

1. Preheat oven to 425°F (220°C). Blend eggs, milk, flour, sugar, cinnamon, and salt.
2. Heat a skillet, melt butter, and arrange apple slices. Pour batter over apples.
3. Bake for 18-20 minutes. Dust with powdered sugar and serve warm.

Blueberry Lemon Scones

Ingredients:

- 2 cups all-purpose flour
- 1/4 cup sugar
- 1 tbsp baking powder
- 1/2 tsp salt
- Zest of 1 lemon
- 1/2 cup cold butter, cubed
- 1 cup fresh blueberries
- 1/2 cup heavy cream
- 1 large egg

Instructions:

1. Preheat oven to 400°F (200°C). Mix flour, sugar, baking powder, salt, and lemon zest.
2. Cut in butter until crumbly, fold in blueberries, then add cream and egg to form a dough.
3. Shape into a disc, cut into wedges, and bake for 15-18 minutes.

Caramelized Onion and Goat Cheese Quiche

Ingredients:

- 1 pie crust
- 2 large onions, thinly sliced
- 2 tbsp butter
- 4 large eggs
- 1 cup milk
- 1/2 cup goat cheese, crumbled
- Salt and pepper, to taste

Instructions:

1. Preheat oven to 375°F (190°C). Sauté onions in butter until caramelized.
2. Place pie crust in a dish, layer with onions and goat cheese.
3. Whisk eggs, milk, salt, and pepper, and pour into the crust.
4. Bake for 35-40 minutes.

Sweet Potato and Kale Hash

Ingredients:

- 2 cups diced sweet potatoes
- 1 tbsp olive oil
- 1 cup chopped kale
- 1/2 tsp smoked paprika
- Salt and pepper, to taste
- 2 large eggs

  Instructions:

1. Heat oil in a skillet and cook sweet potatoes until tender.
2. Add kale, paprika, salt, and pepper, cooking until wilted.
3. Make wells, crack eggs into them, and cook until eggs are set.

Maple Bacon Waffles

Ingredients:

- 2 cups all-purpose flour
- 2 tbsp sugar
- 1 tbsp baking powder
- 1/2 tsp salt
- 2 large eggs
- 1 3/4 cups milk
- 1/2 cup melted butter
- 1/2 cup cooked bacon, crumbled
- Maple syrup, for serving

Instructions:

1. Preheat waffle iron. Mix flour, sugar, baking powder, and salt.
2. Whisk eggs, milk, and butter, then combine with dry ingredients. Fold in bacon.
3. Cook waffles in the iron and serve with maple syrup.

Chorizo and Egg Tacos

Ingredients:

- 1/2 lb chorizo
- 4 large eggs
- 4 small tortillas
- 1/4 cup shredded cheese
- Salsa, for serving

Instructions:

1. Cook chorizo in a skillet.
2. Whisk eggs and scramble with chorizo.
3. Warm tortillas, fill with chorizo mixture, and top with cheese and salsa.

Chocolate Chip Banana Pancakes

Ingredients:

- 1 cup all-purpose flour
- 2 tbsp sugar
- 1 tsp baking powder
- 1/2 tsp baking soda
- Pinch of salt
- 1 ripe banana, mashed
- 1 cup milk
- 1 large egg
- 1/2 cup chocolate chips

Instructions:

1. Mix flour, sugar, baking powder, baking soda, and salt.
2. Whisk banana, milk, and egg, then combine with dry ingredients. Fold in chocolate chips.
3. Cook pancakes on a griddle for 2-3 minutes per side.

Green Smoothie Bowl

Ingredients:

- 1 cup spinach
- 1 frozen banana
- 1/2 cup frozen mango
- 1/2 cup almond milk
- 1/4 cup Greek yogurt
- Toppings: granola, chia seeds, fresh fruit
  Instructions:
1. Blend spinach, banana, mango, almond milk, and yogurt until smooth.
2. Pour into a bowl and add toppings as desired.

Ricotta and Honey Toast with Pistachios

Ingredients:

- 4 slices of bread, toasted
- 1/2 cup ricotta cheese
- 2 tbsp honey
- 2 tbsp chopped pistachios

Instructions:

1. Spread ricotta on each slice of toast.
2. Drizzle with honey and sprinkle with pistachios.

Savory Cheese and Herb Muffins

Ingredients:

- 2 cups all-purpose flour
- 1 tbsp baking powder
- 1/2 tsp salt
- 1 cup shredded cheddar cheese
- 1/4 cup chopped fresh herbs (e.g., parsley, chives)
- 2 large eggs
- 3/4 cup milk
- 1/4 cup melted butter
  Instructions:
1. Preheat oven to 375°F (190°C). Mix flour, baking powder, and salt.
2. Stir in cheese and herbs. Add eggs, milk, and butter to form a batter.
3. Divide into a muffin tin and bake for 18-20 minutes.

Mango Coconut Chia Pudding

Ingredients:

- 1 cup coconut milk
- 3 tbsp chia seeds
- 1 tbsp honey
- 1/2 cup diced mango
  Instructions:
1. Mix coconut milk, chia seeds, and honey in a jar.
2. Refrigerate for 4 hours or overnight, stirring occasionally.
3. Top with diced mango before serving.

Almond Croissant Bread Pudding

Ingredients:

- 4 croissants, cubed
- 2 cups milk
- 3 large eggs
- 1/4 cup sugar
- 1/4 cup sliced almonds
- 1 tsp almond extract

Instructions:

1. Preheat oven to 350°F (175°C). Arrange croissant pieces in a baking dish.
2. Whisk milk, eggs, sugar, and almond extract, then pour over croissants.
3. Sprinkle with almonds and bake for 25-30 minutes.

Cheesy Potato Breakfast Skillet

Ingredients:

- 2 cups diced potatoes
- 1 tbsp olive oil
- 1/2 cup shredded cheddar cheese
- 4 large eggs
- Salt and pepper, to taste
  Instructions:
1. Heat oil in a skillet and cook potatoes until golden and tender.
2. Sprinkle cheese over potatoes and make wells for the eggs.
3. Crack eggs into wells, cover, and cook until eggs are set.

Breakfast Pizza with Arugula

Ingredients:

- 1 pizza crust
- 1/2 cup ricotta cheese
- 1/2 cup shredded mozzarella cheese
- 2 large eggs
- 1 cup fresh arugula
- Olive oil, for drizzling

Instructions:

1. Preheat oven to 450°F (230°C). Spread ricotta on the crust, sprinkle with mozzarella, and crack eggs on top.
2. Bake for 10-12 minutes.
3. Top with arugula and drizzle with olive oil before serving.

Cranberry Walnut Bagels

Ingredients:

- 4 bagels, halved
- 1/4 cup cream cheese
- 2 tbsp dried cranberries
- 2 tbsp chopped walnuts

Instructions:

1. Mix cream cheese with cranberries and walnuts.
2. Spread onto bagel halves and serve.

Breakfast Tacos with Avocado Crema

Ingredients:

- 4 small tortillas
- 4 large scrambled eggs
- 1/2 cup cooked chorizo or bacon
- 1 avocado
- 2 tbsp sour cream
- 1 tbsp lime juice

Instructions:

1. Blend avocado, sour cream, and lime juice to make crema.
2. Fill tortillas with eggs, chorizo, and drizzle with avocado crema.

Zucchini and Parmesan Mini Frittatas

Ingredients:

- 1 cup grated zucchini (squeezed dry)
- 1/2 cup grated Parmesan cheese
- 4 large eggs
- 1/4 cup milk
- Salt and pepper, to taste
- 1/4 tsp garlic powder

Instructions:

1. Preheat oven to 375°F (190°C) and grease a muffin tin.
2. Whisk eggs, milk, salt, pepper, and garlic powder.
3. Stir in zucchini and Parmesan, then divide mixture into muffin cups.
4. Bake for 18-20 minutes until set.

Carrot Cake Oatmeal

Ingredients:

- 1 cup rolled oats
- 2 cups milk or water
- 1/2 cup grated carrot
- 1/4 tsp cinnamon
- 1/4 tsp nutmeg
- 2 tbsp raisins
- 1 tbsp honey or maple syrup
  Instructions:
1. Cook oats, milk, and grated carrot over medium heat until creamy.
2. Stir in cinnamon, nutmeg, raisins, and sweetener. Serve warm.

Turkey Sausage and Spinach Wraps

Ingredients:

- 4 whole wheat tortillas
- 4 turkey sausage links, cooked and crumbled
- 1 cup spinach leaves
- 4 scrambled eggs
- 1/2 cup shredded cheddar cheese

Instructions:

1. Lay tortillas flat and layer with spinach, sausage, eggs, and cheese.
2. Roll up tightly and serve warm or wrap to-go.

Almond Butter and Berry Breakfast Toast

Ingredients:

- 4 slices of whole-grain bread, toasted
- 1/4 cup almond butter
- 1/2 cup mixed fresh berries (e.g., blueberries, strawberries)
- 1 tsp honey
  Instructions:
1. Spread almond butter on each slice of toast.
2. Top with fresh berries and drizzle with honey.

Gingerbread Waffles with Whipped Cream

Ingredients:

- 2 cups all-purpose flour
- 2 tbsp brown sugar
- 1 tbsp baking powder
- 1/2 tsp cinnamon
- 1/2 tsp ground ginger
- 1/4 tsp nutmeg
- 2 large eggs
- 1 3/4 cups milk
- 1/4 cup molasses
- Whipped cream, for serving
  Instructions:
1. Preheat waffle iron. Mix flour, sugar, baking powder, and spices.
2. Whisk eggs, milk, and molasses, then combine with dry ingredients.
3. Cook waffles and serve with whipped cream.

Vegan Breakfast Burritos

Ingredients:

- 4 tortillas
- 1 cup tofu, crumbled
- 1/2 cup black beans
- 1/2 cup diced bell peppers
- 1/2 tsp turmeric
- Salt and pepper, to taste
- 1/4 cup salsa

Instructions:

1. Sauté tofu, beans, and bell peppers with turmeric, salt, and pepper.
2. Fill tortillas with the mixture and add salsa before wrapping.

Sweet Corn and Cheddar Muffins

Ingredients:

- 1 cup cornmeal
- 1 cup all-purpose flour
- 1 tbsp sugar
- 1 tbsp baking powder
- 1/2 tsp salt
- 1 cup shredded cheddar cheese
- 1 cup milk
- 1 large egg
- 1/4 cup melted butter

Instructions:

1. Preheat oven to 375°F (190°C) and line a muffin tin.
2. Mix cornmeal, flour, sugar, baking powder, salt, and cheese.
3. Whisk milk, egg, and butter, then combine with dry ingredients.
4. Divide into muffin cups and bake for 18-20 minutes.

Pear and Almond Danish

Ingredients:

- 1 sheet puff pastry, thawed
- 1 large pear, thinly sliced
- 1/4 cup almond paste
- 2 tbsp sliced almonds
- 1 egg, beaten (for egg wash)
- 1 tbsp honey

Instructions:

1. Preheat oven to 375°F (190°C). Roll out puff pastry and cut into rectangles.
2. Spread almond paste on each rectangle, top with pear slices, and sprinkle with almonds.
3. Brush edges with egg wash and bake for 15-20 minutes. Drizzle with honey before serving.

Scrambled Tofu Breakfast Bowl

Ingredients:

- 1 cup crumbled firm tofu
- 1/2 cup diced vegetables (e.g., bell peppers, onions)
- 1/4 tsp turmeric
- 1/2 tsp garlic powder
- Salt and pepper, to taste
- 1/2 avocado, sliced
- 1/2 cup cooked quinoa or rice
  Instructions:
1. Sauté tofu and vegetables in a skillet with turmeric, garlic powder, salt, and pepper.
2. Serve over quinoa or rice, topped with avocado slices.

Coconut Milk Rice Porridge with Mango

Ingredients:

- 1/2 cup jasmine rice
- 1 cup coconut milk
- 1 cup water
- 2 tbsp sugar
- 1/2 cup diced fresh mango

Instructions:

1. Cook rice with coconut milk, water, and sugar over low heat until creamy.
2. Serve topped with diced mango.

Hearty Lentil and Kale Breakfast Soup

Ingredients:

- 1 cup cooked lentils
- 2 cups vegetable broth
- 1 cup chopped kale
- 1/4 cup diced carrots
- 1/4 tsp smoked paprika
- Salt and pepper, to taste
  Instructions:
1. Simmer lentils, broth, carrots, and paprika for 10 minutes.
2. Add kale and cook until wilted. Adjust seasoning and serve warm.

Pistachio and Raspberry Overnight Oats

Ingredients:

- 1/2 cup rolled oats
- 1/2 cup milk (or plant-based alternative)
- 1 tbsp chopped pistachios
- 1/4 cup fresh raspberries
- 1 tsp honey or maple syrup
  Instructions:
1. Mix oats, milk, pistachios, and sweetener in a jar.
2. Refrigerate overnight. Top with raspberries before serving.

Classic Bagel and Lox Platter

Ingredients:

- 4 bagels, halved and toasted
- 1/2 cup cream cheese
- 8 slices smoked salmon
- 1/4 cup capers
- 1/2 cup thinly sliced red onions
- 1/2 cup sliced cucumbers

Instructions:

1. Spread cream cheese on bagel halves.
2. Top with salmon, capers, onions, and cucumbers.

Chocolate Hazelnut Crepes

Ingredients:

- 1 cup all-purpose flour
- 2 large eggs
- 1 1/2 cups milk
- 2 tbsp melted butter
- 1/4 cup chocolate hazelnut spread
- Optional: whipped cream, chopped hazelnuts

Instructions:

1. Whisk flour, eggs, milk, and butter into a smooth batter.
2. Cook crepes in a non-stick skillet until golden.
3. Spread with chocolate hazelnut spread, roll, and serve with whipped cream and hazelnuts.

www.ingramcontent.com/pod-product-compliance
Lightning Source LLC
LaVergne TN
LVHW081505060526
838201LV00056BA/2948